This book belongs to

Herman
the Hermit Crab

by Cindy W. Hollingsworth

illustrated by Jennifer Tipton Cappoen

Paws and Claws Publishing, LLC
High Point, NC

Author: Cindy W. Hollingsworth
Cover Designer and Illustrator: Jennifer Tipton Cappoen
Editor: Lynn Bemer Coble

PCKids is an imprint of **Paws and Claws Publishing, LLC.**
1589 Skeet Club Road, Suite 102-175
High Point, NC 27265
www.PawsandClawsPublishing.com
info@pawsandclawspublishing.com

ISBN #978-0-9846-724-5-5
Printed in the United States

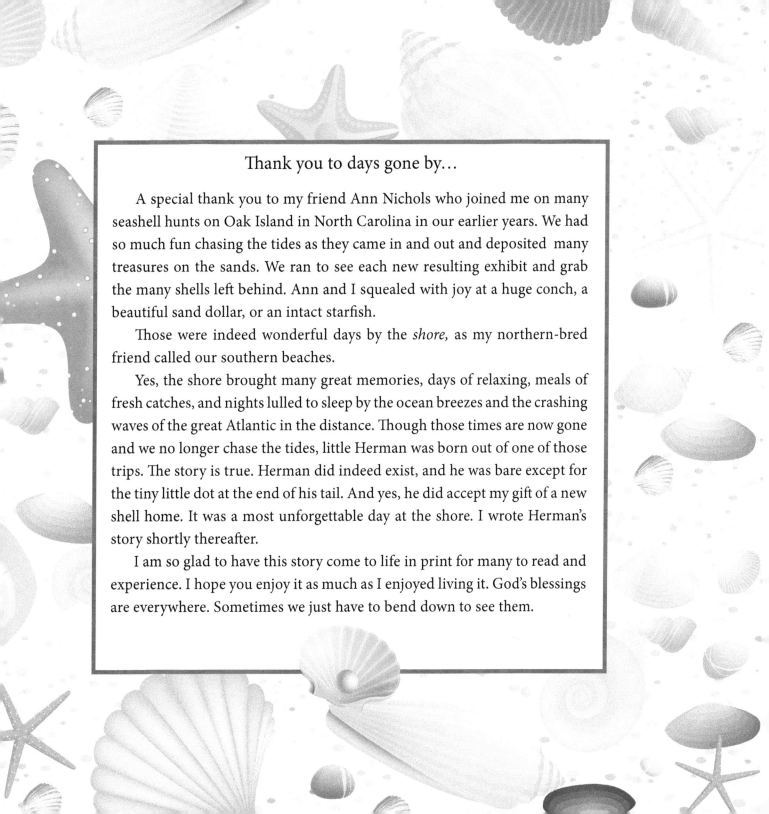

Thank you to days gone by…

A special thank you to my friend Ann Nichols who joined me on many seashell hunts on Oak Island in North Carolina in our earlier years. We had so much fun chasing the tides as they came in and out and deposited many treasures on the sands. We ran to see each new resulting exhibit and grab the many shells left behind. Ann and I squealed with joy at a huge conch, a beautiful sand dollar, or an intact starfish.

Those were indeed wonderful days by the *shore,* as my northern-bred friend called our southern beaches.

Yes, the shore brought many great memories, days of relaxing, meals of fresh catches, and nights lulled to sleep by the ocean breezes and the crashing waves of the great Atlantic in the distance. Though those times are now gone and we no longer chase the tides, little Herman was born out of one of those trips. The story is true. Herman did indeed exist, and he was bare except for the tiny little dot at the end of his tail. And yes, he did accept my gift of a new shell home. It was a most unforgettable day at the shore. I wrote Herman's story shortly thereafter.

I am so glad to have this story come to life in print for many to read and experience. I hope you enjoy it as much as I enjoyed living it. God's blessings are everywhere. Sometimes we just have to bend down to see them.

Once upon a time
 On a visit to the sea,
I found a little hermit crab
 As cute as he could be!

This funny little creature
   In the waters near the sand
Crawled among some tiny seashells,
   Which I'd reached for with my hand.

As I bent to catch the spirals
Shifting slowly with the tide,
My fingers felt some tiny legs
That came from deep inside.

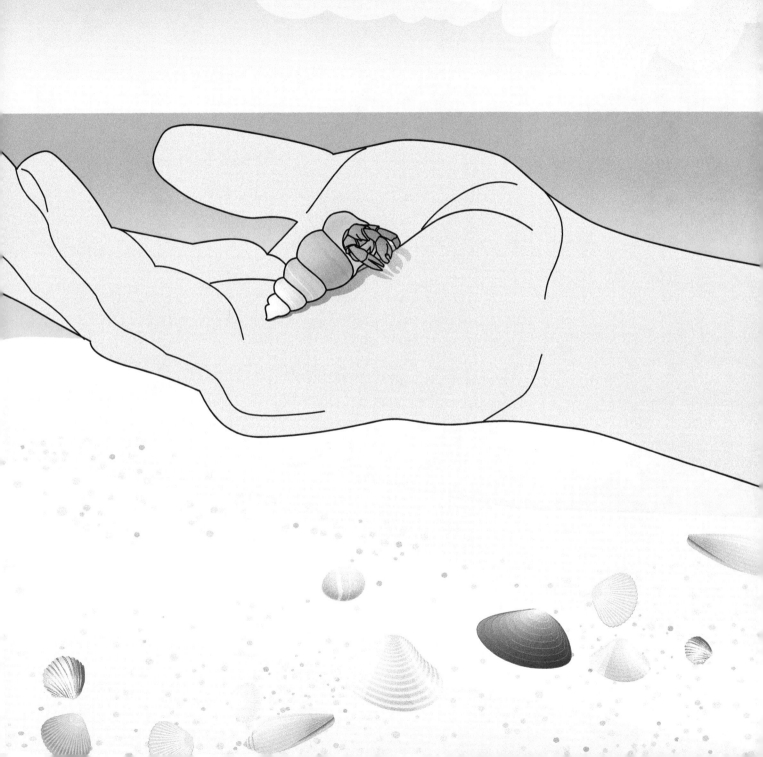

Then suddenly I realized
That in those little shells
Were other tiny hermit crabs
Alive and doing well.

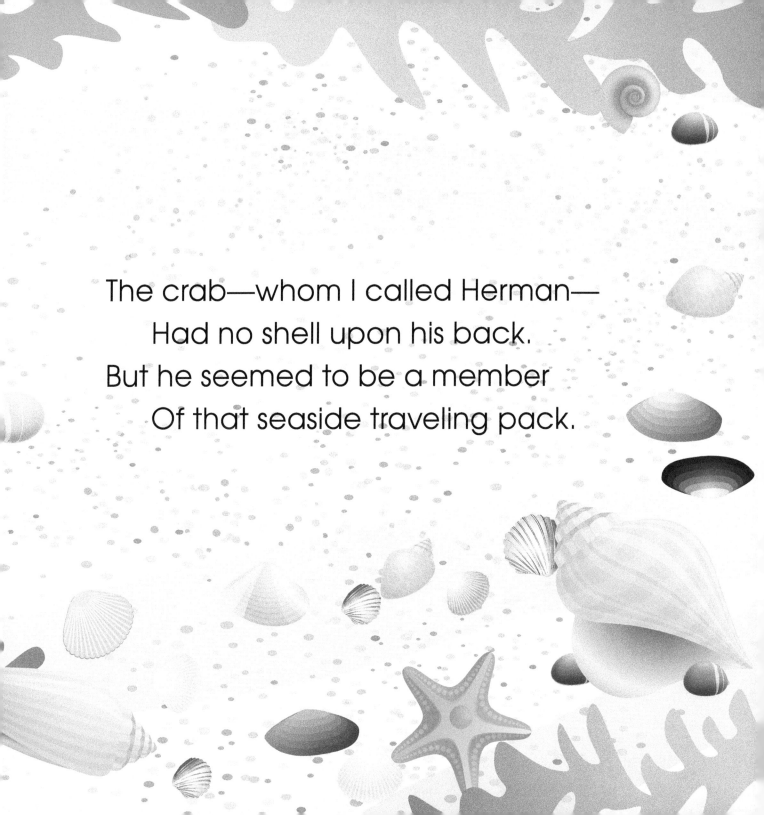

The crab—whom I called Herman—
Had no shell upon his back.
But he seemed to be a member
Of that seaside traveling pack.

I watched with much amusement
As the "shells" walked to and fro.
And right behind came Herman
All bare from head to toe!

But wait. I think I see it.
A tiny, little shell.
A small and teeny-tiny dot
At the end of Herman's tail.

I laughed and
       laughed and
             laughed and laughed.
"Ahhhhhh, poor Herman's gotten fat."
At least I knew he'd grown too much
For the shell that was on his back.

But then I stopped my laughing.
And a sadness filled my heart
For my funny, little sea-crab friend
Who was missing such a part.

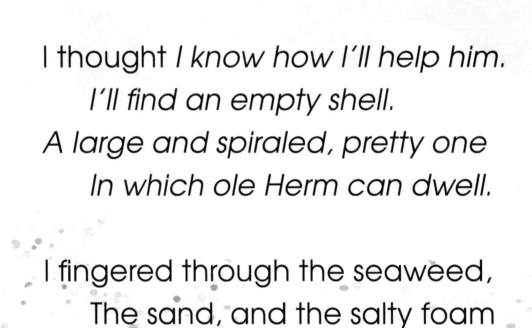

I thought *I know how I'll help him.*
I'll find an empty shell.
A large and spiraled, pretty one
In which ole Herm can dwell.

I fingered through the seaweed,
The sand, and the salty foam
Until I found an empty shell
Just right for Herman's home.

I put it down behind him.
He did not move a bit.
And silently I wondered
If the shell and Herm would fit.

But he had ways of knowing
That I guess I could not see,
'Cause while I bent and stared at him,
He just stared right back at me.

"Oh, come on, Herm," I said aloud,
"You could give the shell a try.
You need a home like all your friends
To keep you safe and dry."

No sooner had I said it
When he backed up to the shell
And seemed to check the inside out
With his tiny little tail.

He stopped and sat really quiet,
His black eyes still on me.
His leggy little body
Still outside and in the sea.

Then whoosh!

He did a rolling flip.

I gave a happy yell,
'Cause when he flipped back over,
He was safe inside my shell.

I love to hunt for seashells
When I go to the beach.
I pick up all the pretty ones
That lie within my reach.

But every time I find a shell,
I wonder in my mind
What tiny creature lived in there—
His home now left behind?

And then I think of Herman
With his seaside traveling pack.

And I reach into my shell bag
And throw a small one back.

THE END

About the Author

Cindy W. Hollingsworth has spent her life dedicated to the dance arts and dance education. She is a graduate of the University of North Carolina at Greensboro with a BS degree in dance. She and her husband owned and operated dance studios in both Virginia and North Carolina for over 43 years. They also founded Dance Troupe, Inc. (DTI), a large national dance seminar and competition company dedicated to the tradition of dance excellence.

Ms. Hollingsworth began writing in her early years. She often wrote scripts for children's plays, pageants, or recital themes. Many of the dance studio recital programs had introductions written by her that were poems related to the themes of the shows. She has written poems for other dance teachers as well and writes biographies and resumes for performers and teachers on request.

Though she never seriously considered writing for publication, she often found her heart called to record in verse or narrative various aspects of life that touched her soul. In 2011, she wrote, sang vocals for, and produced a children's CD for dance and listening called *Songs in My Head*. She wrote the accompanying dance teachers' manual with helpful hints for classroom use of the CD and collaborated on the coloring-book page related to each of the songs. These products and others are available on her website songsinmyhead.net.

Ms. Hollingsworth is a Certified Reiki Master practitioner and teacher. She enjoys the study of healing and stress reduction through holistic and energy techniques. She has developed a love for the theater with recent performances in community theater, having appeared in *Nine to Five—The Musical* playing the role of Roz Keith and in *Arsenic and Old Lace* playing the lead role of one of the spinster sisters, Abby Brewster. She also performed in ensemble and speaking roles in *A Christmas Pudding* and in singing and dancing roles in *The Revue*. She is a noted speaker and lecturer at community organizations, schools, and various local groups. She continues to promote animal rights and the fight to shut down puppy mills and stop the abuse of all types of animals.

According to Ms. Hollingsworth, "My life has always been about dance and creating through movement. Now my creativity has led to other forms of the arts such as songwriting, poetry, and children's rhymes and short stories. Dance will always be my first love. Movement, music, theater, and performing stir my soul to the highest heights of energy and enthusiasm and make living in the world of arts a dream come true. To quote Shakespeare from *As You like It*,

> 'All the world's a stage,
>
> And all the men and women merely players:
>
> They have their exits and their entrances;
>
> And one man in his time plays many parts,
>
> His acts being seven ages....' "

Ms. Hollingsworth resides in Martinsville, Virginia, and lives with her two faithful West Highland Terrier companions Wild Bill and Watson.

About the Artist

Jennifer Tipton Cappoen has a bachelor's degree in fine arts from the University of North Carolina at Greensboro. She has spent more than 28 years honing her skills as an illustrator and a designer for both the educational and Christian publishing markets. Her work has been featured in publications by The Education Center, Inc.; New Day Publishing; True Hope Publishing Inc.; Laurus Books; and Bayard Publishing. She is also the founder and owner of Paws and Claws Publishing, LLC. She lives in Greensboro, North Carolina, with her husband, Andrew, and their four dogs.

CPSIA information can be obtained
at www.ICGtesting.com
Printed in the USA
JSHW051553130123
36148JS00014B/491